ArtNotes

to accompany

History of Art
VOLUME II
REVISED SIXTH EDITION

H. W. Janson
Anthony F. Janson

PEARSON

Prentice
Hall

Upper Saddle River, New Jersey 07458

© 2004 by PEARSON EDUCATION, INC.
Upper Saddle River, New Jersey 07458

ISBN 0-13-184311-7

Printed in the United States of America

Museum credits for fine art photos can be found with the images in the text. Images in the supplement were supplied by SuperStock, Inc. Please note that where we have included artwork in ArtNotes, we have made every effort to secure the same photograph of the art that is found in your text. There are some instances, however, where we had to substitute a slightly different photograph of an object. Please consult your textbook if you are studying the objects for identification purposes.

Contents

Chapter Twelve
The Early Renaissance in Italy

Notes

12-1. Nanni di Banco. *Four Saints (Quattro Coronati).* c. 1410–14. *(page 409)*

_____

_____

_____

_____

_____

_____

_____

_____

_____

_____

_____

12-2. Donatello. *St. Mark.* 1411–13. *(page 410)*

_____

_____

_____

_____

_____

_____

_____

_____

_____

_____

_____

_____

12-3. Donatello. *St. George Tabernacle,* from Or
San Michele, Florence. c. 1415–17. *(page 411)*

12-4. Donatello. *Prophet (Zuccone),* on the
campanile of Florence Cathedral. 1423–25. *(page 412)*

12-5. Donatello. *The Feast of Herod.* c. 1425.
(page 412)

Notes

12-6. Donatello. *David.* c. 1425–30. *(page 413)*

12-7. Donatello. *Equestrian Monument of Gattamelata.* 1445–50. *(page 414)*

12-8. *Mary Magdalen.* c. 1455. *(page 414)*

12-9. Lorenzo Ghiberti. *"Gates of Paradise,"* east doors of the Baptistery of S. Giovanni, Florence. c. 1435. *(page 415)*

12-10. Lorenzo Ghiberti. *The Story of Jacob and Esau,* panel of the *"Gates of Paradise."* c. 1435. *(page 416)*

12-11. Luca della Robbia. *The Resurrection.* 1442–45. *(page 416)*

12-12. Bernardo Rossellino. Tomb of Leonardo
Bruni. c. 1445–50. *(page 417)*

_____

_____

_____

_____

_____

_____

_____

_____

_____

_____

_____

12-13. Desiderio da Settignano. *St. John the
Baptist.* c. 1455–60. *(page 418)*

_____

_____

_____

_____

_____

_____

_____

_____

_____

_____

_____

_____

12-14. Antonio del Pollaiuolo. *Hercules and
Antaeus.* c. 1475. *(page 418)*

_____

_____

_____

_____

_____

_____

_____

_____

_____

_____

_____

_____

12-15. Antonio del Pollaiuolo. *Battle of the Ten Naked Men.* c. 1465–70. *(page 419)*

12-16. Andrea del Verrocchio. *The Doubting of Thomas.* 1465–83. *(page 420)*

12-17. Andrea del Verrocchio. *Equestrian Monument of Colleoni.* c. 1483–88. *(page 420)*

12-18. Jacopo della Quercia. *The Creation of Adam.* c. 1430. *(page 421)*

_____

12-19. *Adam in Paradise,* detail of an ivory diptych. c. 400 A.D. *(page 421)*

_____

12-20. Filippo Brunelleschi. S. Lorenzo, Florence. 1421–69 *(page 422)*

_____

12-21. Plan of S. Lorenzo. Gray area indicates Michelangelo's later addition *(page 422)*

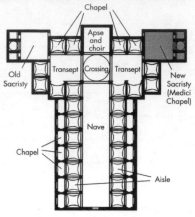

12-22. Filippo Brunelleschi and others. Pazzi Chapel, Sta. Croce, Florence. Begun 1430–33 *(page 424)*

12-23. Plan of the Pazzi Chapel *(page 424)*

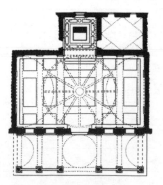

12-24. Longitudinal section of the Pazzi Chapel
(page 424)

12-25. Interior of the Pazzi Chapel *(page 425)*

12-26. Filippo Brunelleschi. Plan of Sta. Maria degli Angeli, Florence. 1434–37 *(page 425)*

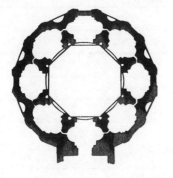

12-27. Michelozzo. Palazzo Medici-Riccardi,
Florence. Begun 1444 *(page 425)*

_____

_____

_____

_____

_____

_____

_____

_____

_____

_____

_____

_____

_____

_____

12-28. Leone Battista Alberti. Palazzo Rucellai,
Florence. 1446–51 *(page 426)*

_____

_____

_____

_____

_____

_____

_____

_____

_____

_____

_____

_____

_____

_____

12-29. Leone Battista Alberti. S. Francesco,
Rimini. Facade designed 1450 *(page 427)*

_____

_____

_____

_____

_____

_____

_____

_____

_____

_____

_____

_____

12-30. S. Francesco, Rimini medal of 1450 by
Matteo dei Pasti. *(page 427)*

_____

_____

_____

_____

_____

_____

_____

_____

_____

_____

_____

12-31. Leone Battista Alberti. S. Maria Novella,
Florence. 1456–1470 *(page 428)*

_____

_____

_____

_____

_____

_____

_____

_____

_____

_____

_____

12-32. Leone Battista Alberti. S. Andrea,
Mantua. Designed 1470 *(page 428)*

_____

_____

_____

_____

_____

_____

_____

_____

_____

_____

_____

12-33. Leone Battista Alberti. Interior of S. Andrea
(page 429)

12-34. Plan of S. Andrea (transept, dome, and choir are later additions) *(page 429)*

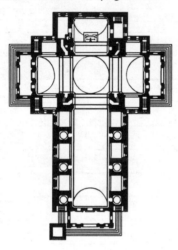

12-35. Giuliano da Sangallo. Sta. Maria delle Carceri, Prato. Begun 1485 *(page 430)*

12-36. Plan of Sta. Maria delle Carceri *(page 430)*

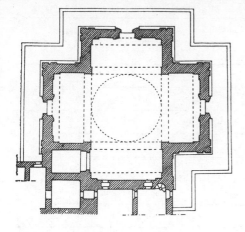

12-37. Interior of Sta. Maria delle Carceri
(page 430)

12-38. Masaccio. *The Holy Trinity with the Virgin,
St. John, and Two Donors.* 1425. *(page 431)*

12-39. Plan of *The Holy Trinity* (page 431)

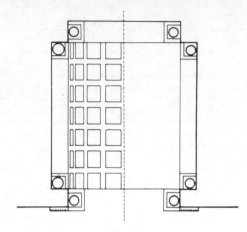

12-40. Left wall of Brancacci Chapel, with frescoes by Masaccio. Sta. Maria del Carmine, Florence *(page 432)*

12-41. Right wall of Brancacci Chapel, with frescoes by Masolino and Filippino Lippi. *(page 433)*

12-42. Masaccio. *The Tribute Money.* c. 1427.
(page 433)

12-43. Masaccio. *The Expulsion from Paradise.*
c. 1427. *(page 434)*

12-44. Masaccio. *Madonna Enthroned.* 1426.
(page 435)

12-45. Fra Angelico. *Deposition.* Probably early 1440s. *(page 436)*

12-46. Domenico Veneziano. *Madonna and Child with Saints.* c. 1455. *(page 437)*

12-47. View into main chapel, with frescoes by Piero della Francesca. S. Francesco, Arezzo *(page 438)*

12-48. Piero della Francesca. *The Discovery and Proving of the True Cross.* c. 1455. *(page 439)*

12-49. Paolo Uccello. *Battle of San Romano.* c. 1455. *(page 439)*

12-50. Andrea del Castagno. *The Last Supper.* c. 1445–50. *(page 440)*

12-51. Andrea del Castagno. *David.* c. 1450–57. *(page 441)*

12-52. Fra Filippo Lippi. *Madonna and Child with the Birth of the Virgin* (The Bartolini Tondo). 1452–53. *(page 441)*

12-53. Sandro Botticelli. *The Birth of Venus.* c. 1480. *(page 442)*

12-54. Sandro Botticelli. *Primavera.* c. 1482. *(page 443)*

BOX. Piero della Francesca. *The Nativity.* Late 15th century. *(page 444)*

12-55. Domenico Ghirlandaio. *An Old Man and His Grandson.* c. 1480. *(page 445)*

12-56. Pietro Perugino. *The Delivery of the Keys.*
1482. *(page 445)*

12-57. Luca Signorelli. *The Rule of the Antichrist.*
1499–1500. *(page 446)*

12-58. Luca Signorelli. *The Damned Cast into
Hell.* 1499–1500. *(page 447)*

12-59. Andrea Mantegna. *St. James Led to His Execution.* c. 1455. *(page 447)*

_____

_____

_____

_____

_____

_____

_____

_____

_____

_____

12-60. Andrea Mantegna. *St. James Led to His Execution.* c. 1455. *(page 448)*

_____

_____

_____

_____

_____

_____

_____

_____

_____

_____

12-61. Andrea Mantegna. *St. Sebastian.* c. 1455–60. *(page 448)*

_____

_____

_____

_____

_____

_____

_____

_____

_____

_____

12-62. Giovanni Bellini. *St. Francis in Ecstasy.*
c. 1485. *(page 449)*

12-63. Giovanni Bellini. *Madonna and Saints.*
1505. *(page 450)*

Chapter Thirteen
The High Renaissance in Italy

Notes

13-1. Leonardo da Vinci. *Adoration of the Magi.*
1481–82. *(page 454)*

_____
_____
_____
_____
_____
_____
_____
_____
_____
_____
_____

13-2. Leonardo da Vinci. *The Virgin of the Rocks.*
c. 1485. *(page 455)*

_____
_____
_____
_____
_____
_____
_____
_____
_____
_____
_____

13-3. Leonardo da Vinci. *The Last Supper.*
c. 1495–98. *(page 455)*

13-4. Leonardo da Vinci. *Mona Lisa.* c. 1503–5.
(page 456)

13-5. Leonardo da Vinci. *Embryo in the Womb.*
c. 1510. *(page 457)*

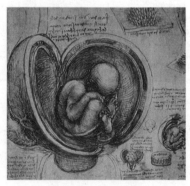

13-6. Leonardo da Vinci. *Project for a Church*
(Ms. B). c. 1490. *(page 457)*

13-7. Donato Bramante. The Tempietto, S. Pietro
in Montorio, Rome. 1502–11 *(page 458)*

13-8. Plan of the Tempietto (after Serlio, in
Regole generali di Architettura). *(page 458)*

13-9. Donato Bramante. Original plan for St. Peter's, Rome. 1506 (after Geymuller) *(page 459)*

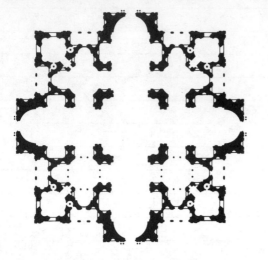

13-10. Caradosso. Bronze medal showing Bramante's design for St. Peter's. 1506. *(page 459)*

13-11. Michelangelo. *Pietà.* c. 1500. *(page 460)*

13-12. Michelangelo. *David.* 1501–4. *(page 461)*

13-13. Michelangelo. *Moses.* c. 1513–15. *(page 462)*

13-14. Michelangelo. *"The Dying Slave."* 1513–16. *(page 462)*

13-15. Michelangelo. *"The Rebellious Slave."*
1513–16. *(page 462)*

13-16. Michelangelo. *Awakening Prisoner.* c. 1525.
(page 463)

BOX. Titian. *Pastoral Concert.* c. 1509–10.
(page 464)

13-17. Interior of the Sistine Chapel showing Michelangelo's ceiling fresco. The Vatican, Rome *(page 465)*

_____

_____

_____

_____

_____

_____

_____

_____

_____

_____

13-18. Michelangelo. *The Creation of Adam,* portion of the Sistine Ceiling. 1508–12. *(page 466)*

_____

_____

_____

_____

_____

_____

_____

_____

_____

_____

_____

13-19. Michelangelo. *The Fall of Man* and *The Expulsion from the Garden of Eden,* portion of the Sistine ceiling. 1508–12. *(page 467)*

_____

_____

_____

_____

_____

_____

_____

_____

_____

_____

13-20. Michelangelo. *The Last Judgment.*
1534–41. *(page 468)*

13-21. Michelangelo. *The Last Judgment*
(detail, with self-portrait) *(page 469)*

13-22. Michelangelo. Tomb of Giuliano de'
Medici. 1524–34. *(page 469)*

13-23. Michelangelo. Vestibule of the Laurentian
Library, Florence. Begun 1524; stairway designed
1558–59 *(page 470)*

13-24. Michelangelo. The Campidoglio (engraving
by Étienne Dupérac, 1569) *(page 470)*

13-25. Plan of the Campidoglio, Rome *(page 471)*

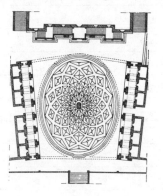

13-26. Michelangelo. Palazzo dei Conservatori,
Campidoglio, Rome. Designed c. 1545 *(page 471)*

13-27. Michelangelo. St. Peter's, Rome, seen
from the west. 1546–64 (dome completed by
Giacomo della Porta, 1590) *(page 472)*

13-28. Michelangelo. Plan for St. Peter's *(page 472)*

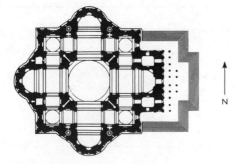

13-29. Raphael. *La Belle Jardinière.* 1507.
(page 473)

_____

_____

_____

_____

_____

_____

_____

_____

_____

_____

_____

13-30. Stanza della Segnatura, with frescoes
by Raphael. 1508–11. *(page 473)*

_____

_____

_____

_____

_____

_____

_____

_____

_____

_____

_____

_____

13-31. Raphael. *The School of Athens.* 1510–11.
(page 474)

_____

_____

_____

_____

_____

_____

_____

_____

_____

_____

_____

_____

13-32. Raphael. *The School of Athens* (detail)
(page 475)

13-33. Raphael. *Galatea.* 1513. *(page 476)*

13-34. Marcantonio Raimondi, after Raphael.
The Judgment of Paris. c. 1520. *(page 476)*

13-35. *The Judgment of Paris.* Roman sarcophagus.
3rd century A.D. *(page 477)*

_____

_____

_____

_____

_____

_____

_____

_____

_____

_____

_____

13-36. Raphael. *Pope Leo X with Giulio de' Medici
and Luigi de' Rossi.* c. 1518. *(page 477)*

_____

_____

_____

_____

_____

_____

_____

_____

_____

_____

_____

13-37. Raphael. *The Sacrifice at Lystra.*
1514–15. *(page 478)*

_____

_____

_____

_____

_____

_____

_____

_____

_____

_____

13-38. Giorgione. *The Tempest.* c. 1505.
(page 479)

13-39. Titian. *Bacchanal.* c. 1518. *(page 480)*

13-40. Titian. *Madonna with Members of the Pesaro Family.* 1526. *(page 481)*

13-41. Titian. *Man with the Glove.* c. 1520.
(page 482)

13-42. Titian. *Pope Paul III and His Grandsons.*
1546. *(page 483)*

13-43. Titian. *Danaë.* c. 1544–46. *(page 484)*

13-44. Titian. *Christ Crowned with Thorns.* c. 1570.
(page 484)

Chapter Fourteen
The Late Renaissance in Italy

Notes

14-1. Rosso Fiorentino. *The Descent from the Cross.* 1521. *(page 489)*

14-2. Jacopo da Pontormo. *The Deposition.* c. 1526–28. *(page 489)*

BOX. Andrea Palladio and Vincenzo Scamozzi. *Stage of the Teatro Olimpico, Vicenza.* c. 1585 (executed by Scamozzi) *(page 490)*

14-3. Parmigianino. *Self-Portrait.* 1524. *(page 491)*

14-4. Parmigianino. *The Madonna with the Long Neck.* c. 1535. *(page 492)*

14-5. Parmigianino. *The Entombment.* c. 1535.
(page 492)

_____

_____

_____

_____

_____

_____

_____

_____

_____

_____

_____

_____

_____

14-6. Agnolo Bronzino. *Allegory of Venus.* c. 1546.
(page 493)

_____

_____

_____

_____

_____

_____

_____

_____

_____

_____

_____

_____

_____

_____

14-7. Giorgio Vasari. *Perseus and Andromeda.*
1570–72. *(page 493)*

_____

_____

_____

_____

_____

_____

_____

_____

_____

_____

_____

_____

14-8. Agnolo Bronzino. *Eleanora of Toledo and Her Son Giovannide' Medici.* c. 1550. *(page 494)*

14-9. Girolamo Savoldo. *St. Matthew and the Angel.* c. 1535. *(page 494)*

14-10. Correggio. *The Assumption of the Virgin.* Dome, Parma Cathedral, Parma, Italy. c. 1525. *(page 495)*

14-11. Correggio. *Jupiter and Io.* c. 1532.
(page 496)

_____

_____

_____

_____

_____

_____

_____

_____

_____

_____

_____

14-12. Jacopo Bassano. *The Adoration of the Shepherds.* 1542–47. *(page 497)*

_____

_____

_____

_____

_____

_____

_____

_____

_____

_____

_____

_____

14-13. Paolo Veronese. *Christ in the House of Levi.* 1573. *(page 498)*

_____

_____

_____

_____

_____

_____

_____

_____

_____

_____

_____

_____

_____

14-14. Jacopo Tintoretto. *Christ Before Pilate.*
1566–67. *(page 499)*

14-15. Jacopo Tintoretto. *The Last Supper.*
1592–94. *(page 500)*

14-16. El Greco. *The Burial of Count Orgaz.*
1586. *(page 501)*

14-17. Chapel with *The Burial of Count Orgaz.*1586. *(page 501)*

_____

_____

_____

_____

_____

_____

_____

_____

_____

_____

_____

14-18. El Greco. *The Agony in the Garden.* 1597–1600. *(page 502)*

_____

_____

_____

_____

_____

_____

_____

_____

_____

_____

_____

14-19. Benvenuto Cellini. *Saltcellar of Francis I.* 1539–43. *(page 503)*

_____

_____

_____

_____

_____

_____

_____

_____

_____

_____

_____

14-20. Francesco Primaticcio. *Stucco Figures.*
c. 1541–45. *(page 504)*

14-21. Giovanni Bologna. *The Abduction of the
Sabine Woman.* Completed 1583. *(page 505)*

14-22. Giulio Romano. Courtyard of the
Palazzo del Te, Mantua. 1527–34 *(page 506)*

14-23. Giorgio Vasari. Loggia of the Palazzo degli Uffizi, Florence (view from the Arno River). Begun 1560 *(page 506)*

14-24. Bartolommeo Ammanati. Courtyard of the Palazzo Pitti, Florence. 1558–70 *(page 507)*

14-25. Jacopo Sansovino.Mint (left) and Library of St. Mark's, Venice. Begun c. 1535/7 *(page 507)*

14-26. Andrea Palladio. Villa Rotonda, Vicenza.
c. 1567–70 *(page 508)*

14-27. Andrea Palladio. S. Giorgio Maggiore,
Venice. Designed 1565 *(page 509)*

14-28. Plan of S. Giorgio Maggiore *(page 509)*

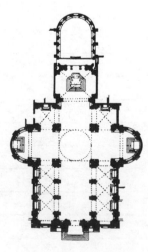

14-29. Giacomo Vignola. Plan of Il Gesù, Rome. 1568 *(page 510)*

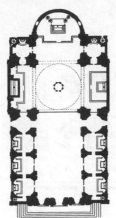

14-30. Andrea Sacchi and Jan Miel. *Urban VIII Visiting Il Gesù.* 1639–41. *(page 510)*

14-31. Giacomo della Porta. Facade of Il Gesù, Rome. c. 1575–84 *(page 511)*

Chapter Fifteen
"Late Gothic" Painting, Sculpture, and the Graphic Arts

15-1. Robert Campin (Master of Flémalle). *Mérode Altarpiece.* c. 1425–30. *(page 513)*

_____

_____

_____

_____

_____

_____

_____

_____

_____

_____

_____

15-2. Hubert and/or Jan van Eyck. *The Crucifixion and The Last Judgment.* c. 1420–25. *(page 515)*

_____

_____

_____

_____

_____

_____

_____

_____

_____

_____

_____

15-3. Hubert and Jan van Eyck. *Ghent Altarpiece*
(open). Completed 1432. *(page 516)*

_____

_____

_____

_____

_____

_____

_____

_____

_____

15-4. *Adam and Eve,* details of *Ghent Altarpiece,*
left and right wings *(page 517)*

_____

_____

_____

_____

_____

_____

_____

_____

_____

_____

15-5. *Adam,* from south transept, Notre-Dame,
Paris. c. 1250. *(page 517)*

_____

_____

_____

_____

_____

_____

_____

_____

_____

_____

15-6. *Ghent Altarpiece* (closed) *(page 518)*

_____

_____

_____

_____

_____

_____

_____

_____

_____

_____

_____

15-7. Jan van Eyck. *Man in a Red Turban (Self-Portrait?).* 1433. *(page 518)*

_____

_____

_____

_____

_____

_____

_____

_____

_____

_____

_____

15-8. Jan van Eyck. *The Arnolfini Portrait.* 1434. *(page 519)*

_____

_____

_____

_____

_____

_____

_____

_____

_____

_____

15-9. Jan van Eyck. *The Arnolfini Portrait* (detail)
(page 519)

_____
_____
_____
_____
_____
_____
_____
_____
_____
_____
_____

15-10. Rogier van der Weyden. *Descent from the Cross.* c. 1435. *(page 520)*

_____
_____
_____
_____
_____
_____
_____
_____
_____
_____
_____

15-11. Rogier van der Weyden. *The Miraflores Altarpiece.* c. 1440–44. *(page 522)*

_____
_____
_____
_____
_____
_____
_____
_____
_____
_____
_____

15-12. Hugo van der Goes. *The Portinari Altarpiece* (open). c. 1476. *(page 523)*

_____

_____

_____

_____

_____

_____

_____

_____

_____

_____

_____

15-13. Geertgen tot Sint Jans. *Nativity.* c. 1490. *(page 523)*

_____

_____

_____

_____

_____

_____

_____

_____

_____

_____

_____

_____

_____

15-14. Hieronymous Bosch. *The Garden of Delights.* c. 1510–15. *(page 524)*

_____

_____

_____

_____

_____

_____

_____

_____

_____

_____

15-15. Conrad Witz. *The Miraculous Draught of Fishes.* 1444. *(page 526)*

15-16. Jean Fouquet. *Étienne Chevalier and St. Stephen,* left wing of the Melun Diptych. c. 1450. *(page 527)*

15-17. Jean Fouquet. *Madonna and Child,* right wing of the Melun Diptych. c. 1450. *(page 527)*

15-18. Jean Fouquet. *The Fall of Jerusalem,*
from Josephus, *Les Antiquités Juda¨ques.*
c. 1470–75. *(page 528)*

15-19. Enguerrand Quarton. *Avignon Pietà.*
c. 1470. *(page 529)*

15-20. Michael Pacher. *St. Wolfgang Altarpiece.*
1471–81. *(page 530)*

15-21. *St. Dorothy.* c. 1420. *(page 531)*

15-22. *Woodcut of St. Christopher,* detail from an *Annunciation* by Jacques Daret (?). c. 1435. *(page 531)*

15-23. Martin Schongauer. *The Temptation of St. Anthony.* c. 1480–90. *(page 533)*

15-24. The Master of the Housebook. *Holy Family by the Rosebush.* c. 1480–90. *(page 533)*

Chapter Sixteen
The Renaissance in the North

Notes

16-1. Lucas Cranach the Elder. *Martin Luther As Junker Jörg.* c. 1521. *(page 534)*

_____

_____

_____

_____

_____

_____

_____

_____

_____

_____

16-2. Matthias Grünewald. *St. Sebastian; The Crucifixion; St. Anthony Abbot;* predella: *Lamentation. Isenheim Altarpiece* (closed). c. 1509/10–15. *(page 536)*

_____

_____

_____

_____

_____

_____

_____

_____

_____

_____

_____

_____

16-3. Matthias Grünewald. *The Annunciation; Madonna and Child with Angels; The Resurrection.* Second view of the *Isenheim Altarpiece.* c. 1509/10–15. *(page 536)*

16-4. Matthias Grünewald. *The Resurrection,* from second view of the *Isenheim Altarpiece* *(page 537)*

16-5. Albrecht Dürer. *Italian Mountains.* c. 1495 or 1505–6. *(page 538)*

16-6. Albrecht Dürer. *The Four Horsemen of the Apocalypse.* c. 1497–98. *(page 539)*

16-7. Albrecht Dürer. *Self-Portrait.* 1500. *(page 539)*

16-8. Albrecht Dürer. *Adam and Eve.* 1504. *(page 539)*

16-9. Albrecht Dürer. *Knight, Death, and Devil.*
1513. *(page 540)*

16-10. Albrecht Dürer. *Melencolia I.* 1514.
(page 540)

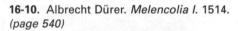

16-11. Albrecht Dürer. *The Four Apostles.*
1523–26. *(page 541)*

16-12. Lucas Cranach the Elder. *The Judgment of Paris.* 1530. *(page 542)*

_____

_____

_____

_____

_____

_____

_____

_____

_____

16-13. Albrecht Altdorfer. *The Battle of Issus.* 1529. *(page 543)*

_____

_____

_____

_____

_____

_____

_____

_____

_____

_____

16-14. Hans Baldung Grien. *Death and the Maiden.* c. 1510. *(page 544)*

_____

_____

_____

_____

_____

_____

_____

_____

_____

_____

_____

_____

16-15. Hans Holbein the Younger. *Erasmus of Rotterdam.* c. 1523. *(page 545)*

16-16. Hans Holbein the Younger. *Henry VIII.* 1540. *(page 546)*

16-17. Nicholas Hilliard. *A Young Man Among Roses.* c. 1588. *(page 546)*

BOX. Marcus Gheeraerts the Younger. *Portrait of Elizabeth I.* c. 1592. *(page 547)*

16-18. Jan Gossaert. *Danaë.* 1527. *(page 549)*

16-19. Joachim Patinir. *Landscape with St. Jerome Removing the Thorn from the Lion's Paw.* c. 1520. *(page 550)*

16-20. Pieter Aertsen. *The Meat Stall.* 1551.
(page 550)

16-21. Pieter Bruegel the Elder. *The Return of the Hunters.* 1565. *(page 551)*

16-22. Pieter Bruegel the Elder. *Peasant Wedding.* c. 1565. *(page 552)*

16-23. Pieter Bruegel the Elder. *The Blind Leading the Blind.* c. 1568. *(page 552)*

16-24. The Château of Chambord (north front), France. Begun 1519 *(page 553)*

16-25. Plan of center portion, Château of Chambord (after Du Cerceau) *(page 553)*

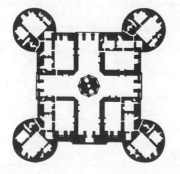

16-26. Gilles Le Breton, Court of the White
Horse, Fontainebleau, 1528–40 *(page 554)*

_____

_____

_____

_____

_____

_____

_____

_____

_____

16-27. Pierre Lescot. Square Court of the
Louvre, Paris. Begun 1546 *(page 554)*

_____

_____

_____

_____

_____

_____

_____

_____

_____

_____

16-28. Jean Goujon. Reliefs from the Fontaine des
Innocents, Paris (dismantled). 1548–49. *(page 555)*

_____

_____

_____

_____

_____

_____

_____

_____

_____

_____

16-29. Francesco Primaticcio and Germain
Pilon. Tomb of Henry II. 1563–70. *(page 556)*

_____

_____

_____

_____

_____

_____

_____

_____

_____

16-30. Germain Pilon. *Gisants* of the king and
queen, detail of the Tomb of Henry II *(page 556)*

_____

_____

_____

_____

_____

_____

_____

_____

_____

16-31. Robert Smythson, Allen Maynard, and others.
Longleat, Wiltshire, England. 1572–80 *(page 557)*

_____

_____

_____

_____

_____

_____

_____

_____

16-32. Plan of Longleat House, Wiltshire (after a plan from Sir Bannister Fletcher's *A History of Architecture*) *(page 557)*

Chapter Seventeen
The Baroque in Italy and Spain

Notes

17-1. Contarelli Chapel, S. Luigi dei Francesi, Rome *(page 559)*

17-2. Caravaggio. *The Calling of St. Matthew.* c. 1599–1602. *(page 560)*

17-3. Jusepe Ribera. *St. Jerome and the Angel of Judgment.* 1626. *(page 562)*

17-4. Artemisia Gentileschi. *Judith and Her Maidservant with the Head of Holofernes.* c.1625. *(page 563)*

17-5. Annibale Carracci. Ceiling fresco. 1597–1601. *(page 564)*

17-6. Annibale Carracci. Ceiling fresco (detail).
Gallery, Palazzo Farnese *(page 565)*

17-7. Annibale Carracci. *Landscape with the
Flight into Egypt.* c. 1603. *(page 565)*

17-8. Giovanni Lanfranco. *Annunciation.* c. 1616.
(page 566)

17-9. Domenichino. *St. Cecilia.* c. 1617–18. *(page 566)*

17-10. Guido Reni. Aurora. 1613. *(page 567)*

17-11. Guercino. *Aurora.* 1621–23. *(page 567)*

17-12. Pietro da Cortona. *The Glorification of the Reign of Urban VIII.* 1633–39. *(page 568)*

BOX. Caravaggio. *The Musicians.* c. 1595. *(page 569)*

17-13. Giovanni Battista Gaulli. *Triumph of the Name of Jesus.* 1672–85. *(page 570)*

17-14. Luca Giordano. *The Abduction of Europa.* 1686. *(page 570)*

_____

_____

_____

_____

_____

_____

_____

_____

_____

_____

17-15. Aerial view of St. Peter's, Rome. Nave and facade by Carlo Maderno, 1607–15; colonnade by Gianlorenzo Bernini, designed 1657 *(page 571)*

_____

_____

_____

_____

_____

_____

_____

_____

_____

_____

_____

_____

17-16. Carlo Maderno. Nave, with Bernini's Tabernacle (1624–33) at crossing, St. Peter's, Rome *(page 572)*

_____

_____

_____

_____

_____

_____

_____

_____

_____

_____

_____

17-17. Pietro da Cortona. Facade of Ss. Luca e
Martina, Rome. c. 1635–50 *(page 572)*

17-18. Francesco Borromini. Facade of S. Carlo
alle Quattro Fontane, Rome. 1665–67 *(page 573)*

17-19. Plan of S. Carlo alle Quattro Fontane.
Begun 1638 *(page 573)*

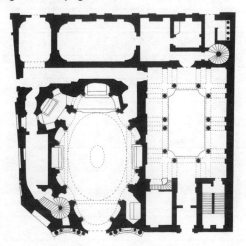

17-20. Dome of S. Carlo alle Quattro Fontane
(page 573)

17-21. Francesco Borromini. Section, S. Ivo,
Rome. Begun 1642 *(page 574)*

17-22. Dome of S. Ivo *(page 574)*

17-23 Francesco Borromini. S. Agnese in Piazza
Navona, Rome. 1653–63 *(page 575)*

_____

_____

_____

_____

_____

_____

_____

_____

_____

_____

_____

17-24. Guarino Guarini. Facade of Palazzo
Carignano, Turin. Begun 1679 *(page 576)*

_____

_____

_____

_____

_____

_____

_____

_____

_____

_____

_____

_____

17-25. Plan of Palazzo Carignano *(page 576)*

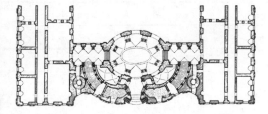

_____

_____

_____

_____

_____

_____

_____

_____

_____

_____

17-26. Guarino Guarini. Dome of the Chapel of the Holy Shroud, Turin Cathedral. 1668–94 *(page 576)*

17-27. Plan of the Chapel of the Holy Shroud and of the dome *(page 576)*

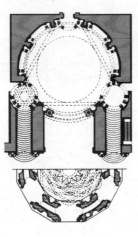

17-28. Gianlorenzo Bernini. *David.* 1623. *(page 577)*

17-29. Gianlorenzo Bernini. *The Ecstasy of St. Theresa.* 1645–52. *(page 578)*

17-30. *The Cornaro Chapel.* 18th-century painting. *(page 579)*

17-31. Alessandro Algardi. *The Meeting of Pope Leo I and Attila.* 1646. *(page 580)*

17-32. Juan Sanchez Cotán. *Quince, Cabbage, Melon, and Cucumber.* c. 1602. *(page 581)*

17-33. Diego Velázquez. *The Water Carrier of Seville.* c. 1619. *(page 582)*

17-34. Diego Velázquez. *Pope Innocent X.* 1650. *(page 583)*

17-35. Diego Velázquez. *The Maids of Honor.*
1656. *(page 584)*

17-36. Francisco de Zurbarán. *St. Serapion.*
1628. *(page 585)*

17-37. Bartolomé Esteban Murillo. *Virgin and
Child.* c. 1675–80. *(page 585)*

Chapter Eighteen
The Baroque in Flanders and Holland

18-1. Peter Paul Rubens. *The Raising of the Cross.* 1609–10. *(page 587)*

18-2. Peter Paul Rubens. *Marie de' Medici, Queen of France, Landing in Marseilles.* 1622–23. *(page 588)*

18-3. Peter Paul Rubens. *The Garden of Love.*
c. 1638. *(page 588)*

18-4. Peter Paul Rubens. *Landscape with the
Château Steen.* 1636. *(page 589)*

18-5. Anthony van Dyck. *Rinaldo and Armida.*
1629. *(page 589)*

18-6. Anthony van Dyck. *Portrait of Charles I Hunting.* c. 1635. *(page 590)*

18-7. Jacob Jordaens. *Homage to Pomona (Allegory of Fruitfulness).* c. 1623. *(page 590)*

18-8. Jan Brueghel the Elder. *Allegory of Earth.* c. 1618. *(page 591)*

18-9. Frans Snyders. *Market Stall.* 1614.
(page 592)

_____

_____

_____

_____

_____

_____

_____

_____

_____

18-10. Hendrick Terbrugghen. *The Calling of
St. Matthew.* 1621. *(page 592)*

_____

_____

_____

_____

_____

_____

_____

_____

_____

_____

18-11. Frans Hals. *The Jolly Toper.* c. 1628–30.
(page 593)

_____

_____

_____

_____

_____

_____

_____

_____

_____

_____

18-12. Frans Hals. *Malle Babbe.* c. 1650. *(page 593)*

18-13. Frans Hals. *The Women Regents of the Old Men's Home at Haarlem.* 1664. *(page 593)*

18-14. Judith Leyster. *Boy Playing a Flute.* 1630–35. *(page 594)*

18-15. Rembrandt. *The Blinding of Samson.* 1636.
(page 594)

18-16. Rembrandt. *The Night Watch (The Company of Captain Frans Banning Cocq).* 1642. *(page 595)*

18-17. Rembrandt. *Christ Preaching.* c. 1652. *(page 596)*

18-18. Rembrandt. *Self-Portrait.* 1658. *(page 596)*

18-19. Rembrandt. *The Return of the Prodigal Son.* c. 1665. *(page 597)*

18-20. Jan van Goyen. *Pelkus-Poort.* 1646. *(page 598)*

18-21. Aelbert Cuyp. *View of the Valkhof at Nijmegen.* c. 1655–65. *(page 598)*

_____

_____

_____

_____

_____

_____

_____

_____

_____

_____

18-22. Jacob van Ruisdael. *The Jewish Cemetery.* 1655–60. *(page 599)*

_____

_____

_____

_____

_____

_____

_____

_____

_____

_____

_____

18-23. PieterSaenredam. *Interior of the Choir of St. Bavo's Church at Haarlem.* 1660. *(page 599)*

_____

_____

_____

_____

_____

_____

_____

_____

_____

_____

18-24. Willem Claesz. Heda. *Still Life.* 1634.
(page 600)

_____

_____

_____

_____

_____

_____

_____

_____

_____

_____

_____

_____

18-25. Jan de Heem. *Still Life with Parrots.*
Late 1640s. *(page 601)*

_____

_____

_____

_____

_____

_____

_____

_____

_____

_____

_____

_____

18-26. Rachel Ruysch. *Flower Still Life.* After
1700. *(page 602)*

_____

_____

_____

_____

_____

_____

_____

_____

_____

_____

_____

_____

18-27. Jan Steen. *The Feast of St. Nicholas.*
c. 1660–65. *(page 603)*

18-28. Jan Vermeer. *Woman Holding a Balance.*
c. 1664. *(page 604)*

18-29. Jan Vermeer. *The Letter.* 1666. *(page 605)*

Chapter Nineteen
The Baroque in France and England

19-1. Jacques Callot. *Hangman's Tree,* from *Great Miseries of War.* 1633. *(page 607)*

19-2. Georges de La Tour. *Joseph the Carpenter.* c. 1645. *(page 607)*

19-3. Louis Le Nain. *Peasant Family.* c. 1640. *(page 608)*

19-4. Nicolas Poussin. *Cephalus and Aurora.* c. 1630. *(page 609)*

19-5. Nicolas Poussin. *The Abduction of the Sabine Women.* c. 1633–34. *(page 609)*

19-6. Nicolas Poussin. *The Birth of Bacchus.*
c. 1657. *(page 610)*

19-7. Claude Lorraine. *A Pastoral Landscape.*
c. 1650. *(page 611)*

19-8. Simon Vouet. *The Toilet of Venus.* c. 1640.
(page 611)

BOX. Laurent de la Hyre. *Allegory of Music.*
1645. *(page 612)*

19-9. François Mansart. Vestibule of the Château
of Maisons. 1642–50 *(page 614)*

19-10. Claude Perrault. East Front of the Louvre,
Paris. 1667–70 *(page 614)*

19-11. Louis Le Vau and Jules Hardouin-Mansart. Garden Front of the center block of the Palace of Versailles. 1669–85 *(page 615)*

19-12. Hardouin-Mansart, Lebrun, and Coysevox. Galerie des Glaces (Hall of Mirrors), Palace of Versailles *(page 616)*

19-13. Hardouin-Mansart, Lebrun, and Coysevox. Salon de la Guerre, Palace of Versailles. Begun 1678 *(page 616)*

19-14. Charles Rivière. *Perspective View of the Château and Gardens of Versailles.* Lithograph after an 1860 photograph *(page 617)*

19-15. Jules Hardouin-Mansart. Church of the Invalides, Paris. 1680–91 *(page 617)*

19-16. Plan of the Church of the Invalides *(page 617)*

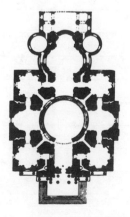

19-17. Gianlorenzo Bernini. *Model for Equestrian Statue of Louis XIV.* 1670. *(page 618)*

19-18. Antoine Coysevox. *Charles Lebrun.* 1676. *(page 618)*

19-19. Pierre-Paul Puget. *Milo of Crotona.* 1671–83. *(page 619)*

BOX. Sir Peter Lely and Studio. *Portrait of Nell Gwyn As Venus with Her Son Charles Beauclerk As Cupid.* 17th century. *(page 620)*

_____

_____

_____

_____

_____

_____

_____

_____

_____

_____

_____

19-20. Inigo Jones. West front of the Banqueting House, Whitehall Palace, London. 1619–22 *(page 621)*

_____

_____

_____

_____

_____

_____

_____

_____

_____

_____

_____

_____

_____

19-21. Sir Christopher Wren. Facade of St. Paul's Cathedral, London. 1675–1710 *(page 621)*

_____

_____

_____

_____

_____

_____

_____

_____

_____

_____

_____

19-22. Plan of St. Paul's Cathedral *(page 621)*

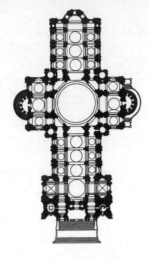

19-23. Interior of St. Paul's Cathedral *(page 622)*

19-24. William Clere. The "Great Model" for
St. Paul's Cathedral by Sir Christopher Wren. 1673.
(page 622)

19-25. Sir John Vanbrugh. Blenheim Palace, Woodstock, England. Begun 1705 *(page 623)*

_____

_____

_____

_____

_____

_____

_____

_____

_____

_____

_____

Chapter Twenty
The Rococo

20-1. Robert de Cotte. Grand Salon of the Hôtel de Bourvallais, Paris. 1717 *(page 625)*

20-2. Claude Michel, known as Clodion. *Satyr and Bacchante.* c. 1775. *(page 625)*

20-3. Jean-Baptiste Pigalle. Tomb of the
Maréchal de Saxe. 1753–76. *(page 626)*

_____

_____

_____

_____

_____

_____

_____

_____

_____

_____

20-4. Jean-Antoine Watteau. *A Pilgrimage to
Cythera.* 1717. *(page 627)*

_____

_____

_____

_____

_____

_____

_____

_____

_____

_____

_____

20-5. Jean-Antoine Watteau. *Gilles and Four
Other Characters from the Commedia dell'Arte
(Pierrot).* c. 1719. *(page 627)*

_____

_____

_____

_____

_____

_____

_____

_____

_____

20-6. François Boucher. *The Toilet of Venus.*
1751. *(page 628)*

20-7. Jean-Honoré Fragonard. *Bathers.*c. 1765.
(page 628)

20-8. Jean-Baptiste-Siméon Chardin. *Back
from the Market.* 1739. *(page 629)*

20-9. Jean-Baptiste-Siméon Chardin. *Kitchen Still Life.* c. 1731. *(page 629)*

20-10. Marie-Louise-Élisabeth Vigée-Lebrun. *The Duchesse de Polignac.* 1783. *(page 630)*

20-11. William Hogarth. *The Orgy,* Scene III of *The Rake's Progress.* c. 1734. *(page 631)*

20-12. William Hogarth. *He Revels (The Orgy),* Scene III of *The Rake's Progress.* 1735. *(page 631)*

20-13. Thomas Gainsborough. *Robert Andrews and His Wife.* c. 1748–50. *(page 632)*

20-14. Thomas Gainsborough. *Mrs. Siddons.* 1785. *(page 633)*

20-15. Sir Joshua Reynolds. *Mrs. Siddons As the Tragic Muse.* 1784. *(page 633)*

20-16. Louis-François Roubiliac. *George Frideric Handel.* 1738. *(page 634)*

20-17. Johann Fischer von Erlach. Facade of St. Charles Borromaeus (Karlskirche), Vienna. 1716–37 *(page 635)*

20-18. Plan of St. Charles Borromaeus
(page 635)

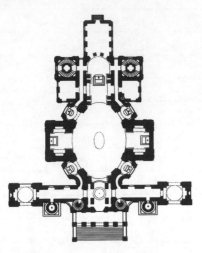

BOX. Jean Antoine Watteau. *Mezzetin.* 1718.
(page 636)

20-19. Jakob Prandtauer. Monastery Church,
Melk, Austria. Begun 1702 *(page 637)*

20-20. Balthasar Neumann. Kaisersaal, Residenz, Würzburg,Germany. 1719–44. Frescoes by Giovanni Battista Tiepolo, 1751-52 *(page 638)*

20-21. Dominikus Zimmermann. Interior of Die Wies, Upper Bavaria, Germany. 1745–54 *(page 639)*

20-22. Plan of Die Wies *(page 639)*

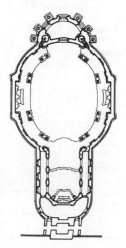

BOX. Sir Joshua Reynolds. *Garrick Between Tragedy and Comedy.* 1761. *(page 640)*

20-23. Giovanni Battista Tiepolo. Ceiling fresco (detail). 1751. Kaisersaal, Residenz, Würzburg *(page 641)*

20-24. Giovanni Battista Tiepolo. *The Marriage of Frederick Barbarossa*(partial view). 1752. *(page 642)*

20-25. Corrado Giaquinto. *Justice and Peace.*
c. 1753–54. *(page 642)*

_____

_____

_____

_____

_____

_____

_____

_____

_____

_____

20-26. Canaletto. *The Bucintoro at the Molo.*
c. 1732. *(page 643)*

_____

_____

_____

_____

_____

_____

_____

_____

_____

_____

_____

20-27. Giovanni Battista Piranesi. *Tower with
Bridges,* from *Prison Caprices.* 1760–61. *(page 643)*

_____

_____

_____

_____

_____

_____

_____

_____

_____

_____

_____

Chapter Twenty-One
Neoclassicism and Romanticism

Notes

21-1. Jean-Baptiste Greuze. *The Village Bride.* 1761. *(page 673)*

_____
_____
_____
_____
_____
_____
_____
_____
_____
_____
_____

21-2. Jacques-Louis David. *The Death of Socrates.* 1787. *(page 674)*

_____
_____
_____
_____
_____
_____
_____
_____
_____
_____

21-3. Jacques-Louis David. *The Death of Marat.* 1793. *(page 675)*

21-4. Benjamin West. *The Death of General Wolfe.* 1770. *(page 676)*

21-5. John Singleton Copley. *Paul Revere.* c. 1768–70. *(page 677)*

21-6. Francis Xavier Vispré (attr.). *Portrait of Louis-François Roubiliac.* c. 1750. *(page 677)*

21-7. John Singleton Copley. *Watson and the Shark.* 1778. *(page 678)*

21-8. Angelica Kauffmann. *The Artist in the Character of Design Listening to the Inspiration of Poetry.* 1782. *(page 679)*

21-9. George Stubbs. *Lion Attacking a Horse.*
1770. *(page 679)*

_____

_____

_____

_____

_____

_____

_____

_____

_____

_____

21-10. Alexander Cozens. *Landscape,* from *A New
Method of Assisting the Invention in Drawing Original
Compositions of Landscape.* 1784–86. *(page 680)*

_____

_____

_____

_____

_____

_____

_____

_____

_____

_____

_____

_____

21-11. Thomas Banks. *The Death of Germanicus.*
1774. *(page 681)*

_____

_____

_____

_____

_____

_____

_____

_____

_____

_____

_____

21-12. Jean-Antoine Houdon. *Voltaire Seated.*
1781. *(page 682)*

21-13. Jean-Antoine Houdon. *George Washington.* 1788–92. *(page 682)*

BOX. Johann Heinrich Wilhelm Tischbein.
Goethe in the Campagna. 1787. *(page 683)*

21-14. Lord Burlington and William Kent. Chiswick House, near London. Begun 1725 *(page 684)*

_____

_____

_____

_____

_____

_____

_____

_____

_____

_____

21-15. Henry Flitcroft and Henry Hoare. Landscape garden with Temple of Apollo, Stourhead, England. 1744–65 *(page 685)*

_____

_____

_____

_____

_____

_____

_____

_____

_____

_____

21-16. Jacques-Germain Soufflot. The Panthéon (Ste.-Geneviève), Paris. 1757–92 *(page 686)*

_____

_____

_____

_____

_____

_____

_____

_____

_____

_____

_____

21-17. Étienne-Louis Boullée. *Project for a Memorial to Isaac Newton.* 1784. *(page 687)*

21-18. Claude-Nicolas Ledoux. Barrière de Villette (after restoration), Paris. 1785–89 *(page 687)*

BOX. Thomas Gainsborough. *Portrait of Johann Christian Fischer.* 1780. *(page 688)*

21-19. Robert Adam. The Library, Kenwood, London. 1767–69 *(page 689)*

_____

_____

_____

_____

_____

_____

_____

_____

_____

_____

_____

21-20. Thomas Jefferson. Monticello, Charlottesville, Virginia. 1770–84; 1796–1806 *(page 690)*

_____

_____

_____

_____

_____

_____

_____

_____

_____

_____

_____

21-21. Plan of Monticello *(page 690)*

_____

_____

_____

_____

_____

_____

_____

_____

_____

_____

_____

21-22. Francisco Goya. *The Sleep of Reason Produces Monsters,* from Los Caprichos. c. 1798. *(page 691)*

21-23. Francisco Goya. *The Family of Charles IV.* 1800. (page 692)

21-24. Francisco Goya. *The Second of May, 1808.* 1814. *(page 693)*

21-25. Francisco Goya. *The Third of May, 1808.*
1814. *(page 693)*

21-26. Anne-Louis Girodet-Trioson. *The Funeral of
Atala.* 1808. *(page 695)*

21-27. Antoine-Jean Gros. *Napoleon in the Pesthouse
at Jaffa, 11 March 1799.* 1804. *(page 695)*

21-28. Théodore Géricault.*The Raft of the "Medusa."* 1818–19. *(page 696)*

21-29. Théodore Géricault. *The Madman.* 1821–24. *(page 697)*

21-30. Jean-Auguste-Dominique Ingres. *Odalisque with a Slave.* 1839–40. *(page 698)*

21-31. Jean-Auguste-Dominique Ingres. *Louis-François Bertin.* 1832. *(page 698)*

_____

_____

_____

_____

_____

_____

_____

_____

_____

_____

_____

21-32. Jean-Auguste-Dominique Ingres. *Louis-François Bertin.* 1832. *(page 698)*

_____

_____

_____

_____

_____

_____

_____

_____

_____

_____

_____

_____

_____

21-33. Eugène Delacroix. *The Death of Sardanapalus.* 1827. *(page 699)*

_____

_____

_____

_____

_____

_____

_____

_____

_____

_____

_____

21-34. Eugène Delacroix. *Women of Algiers.*
1834. *(page 700)*

21-35. Eugène Delacroix. *The Abduction of
Rebecca.* 1846. *(page 701)*

21-36. Honoré Daumier. *It's Safe to Release
This One!* 1834. *(page 702)*

21-37. Honoré Daumier. *The Third-Class Carriage.* c. 1862. *(page 702)*

21-38. Camille Corot. *View of Rome: The Bridge and Castel Sant'Angelo with the Cupola of St. Peter's.* 1826–27. *(page 703)*

21-39. Camille Corot. *Morning: Dance of the Nymphs.* 1850. *(page 704)*

21-40. Théodore Rousseau. *A Meadow Bordered by Trees.* c. 1840–45. *(page 704)*

21-41. Jean-François Millet. *The Sower.* c. 1850. *(page 705)*

21-42. Rosa Bonheur. *Plowing in the Nivernais.* 1849. *(page 706)*

21-43. John Henry Fuseli. *The Nightmare.* c. 1790. *(page 706)*

_____

_____

_____

_____

_____

_____

_____

_____

_____

_____

21-44. William Blake. *The Ancient of Days,* frontispiece of *Europe, A Prophesy.* 1794. *(page 707)*

_____

_____

_____

_____

_____

_____

_____

_____

_____

_____

21-45. Taddeo Zuccaro. *The Conversion of St. Paul* (detail). c. 1555. *(page 707)*

_____

_____

_____

_____

_____

_____

_____

_____

_____

_____

_____

21-46. John Constable. *The Haywain.* 1821. *(page 708)*

21-47. John Constable. *Salisbury Cathedral from the Meadows.* 1829–34. *(page 709)*

21-48. Joseph Mallord William Turner. *The Slave Ship.* 1840. *(page 710)*

21-49. Joseph Mallord William Turner. *Rain, Steam and Speed—The Great Western Railway.* 1844. *(page 710)*

_____

_____

_____

_____

_____

_____

_____

_____

_____

21-50. John Cotman. *Durham Cathedral.* 1805. *(page 711)*

_____

_____

_____

_____

_____

_____

_____

_____

_____

_____

_____

21-51. Caspar David Friedrich. *Abbey in an Oak Forest.* 1809–10. *(page 712)*

_____

_____

_____

_____

_____

_____

_____

_____

_____

_____

21-52. Caspar David Friedrich. *The Polar Sea.*
1824. *(page 713)*

21-53. Philipp Otto Runge. *Morning.* 1808.
(page 713)

BOX. Eugène Delacroix. *Mephistopheles
Appears Before Faust.* 1826–27. *(page 714)*

21-54. Friedrich Overbeck. *Italia and Germania.* 1811–28. *(page 715)*

21-55. William Sidney Mount. *Dancing on the Barn Floor.* 1831. *(page 716)*

21-56. Thomas Cole. *View of Schroon Mountain, Essex County, New York, After a Storm.* 1838. *(page 717)*

21-57. George Caleb Bingham. *Fur Traders Descending the Missouri.* c. 1845. *(page 717)*

21-58. Antonio Canova. Tomb of the Archduchess Maria Christina. 1798–1805. *(page 718)*

21-59. Antonio Canova. *Pauline Borghese As Venus.* 1808. *(page 719)*

21-60. Bertel Thorvaldsen. *Venus.* 1813–16.
(page 720)

_____

_____

_____

_____

_____

_____

_____

_____

_____

_____

_____

21-61. François Rude. *La Marseillaise.* 1833–36.
(page 721)

_____

_____

_____

_____

_____

_____

_____

_____

_____

_____

_____

Jean-Auguste-Dominique Ingres. *Cherubini and the Muse of Lyric Poetry.* 1842. *(page 723)*

_____

_____

_____

_____

_____

_____

_____

_____

_____

_____

_____

21-62. Antoine-Louis Barye. *Tiger Devouring a Gavial of the Ganges.* 1831–32. *(page 724)*

21-63. Auguste Préault. *Tuerie (Slaughter).* 1834. *(page 724)*

21-64. Jean-Baptiste Carpeaux. *The Dance.* 1867–69. *(page 725)*

21-65. Auguste Bartholdi. *Statue of Liberty (Liberty Enlightening the World).* 1875–84. *(page 726)*

21-66. Karl Friedrich Schinkel. Altes Museum, Berlin. 1824–28 *(page 727)*

21-67. Leo von Klenze. Walhalla, near Regensburg, Germany. 1821–42 *(page 728)*

21-68. Horace Walpole, with William Robinson
and others. Strawberry Hill, Twickenham,
England. 1749–77 *(page 728)*

21-69. Interior of Strawberry Hill *(page 728)*

21-70. John Nash. The Royal Pavilion, Brighton,
England. 1815–18 *(page 729)*

21-71. Benjamin Latrobe. Baltimore Cathedral
(Basilica of the Assumption), Baltimore, Maryland.
Begun 1805 *(page 730)*

21-72. Interior of Baltimore Cathedral *(page 730)*

21-73. Sir John Soane. Consols' Office, Bank of
England, London. 1794. Destroyed *(page 730)*

21-74. Sir Charles Barry and A. N. Welby
Pugin. The Houses of Parliament, London.
Begun 1836 *(page 731)*

21-75. Charles Garnier. Grand Staircase, the Opéra,
Paris. 1861–74 *(page 732)*

21-76. Plan of the Opéra *(page 732)*

21-77. The Opéra *(page 732)*

21-78. François-Honoré Jacob-Desmalter (after a design by Charles Percier and Pierre-François Fontaine). Bedroom of Empress Joséphine Bonaparte. c. 1810. *(page 733)*

21-79. Joseph Nicéphore Niépce. *View from His Window at Le Gras.* 1826. *(page 734)*

21-80. Louis-Jacques-Mandé Daguerre. *Still Life.* 1837. *(page 735)*

21-81. William Henry Fox Talbot. *Sailing Craft.* c. 1845. *(page 735)*

21-82. Nadar.*Sarah Bernhardt.* 1859. *(page 736)*

21-83. Honoré Daumier. *Nadar Elevating Photography to the Height of Art.* 1862. *(page 736)*

_____

_____

_____

_____

_____

_____

_____

_____

_____

_____

21-84. Timothy O'Sullivan. *Ancient Ruins in the Cañon de Chelle, N.M., in a Niche 50 Feet above the Present Cañon Bed* (now Canyon de Chelly National Monument, Arizona). 1873. *(page 736)*

_____

_____

_____

_____

_____

_____

_____

_____

_____

_____

_____

_____

21-85. *Tsar Cannon Outside the Spassky Gate, Moscow* (cast 1586; presently inside the Kremlin). Second half of 19th century. *(page 737)*

_____

_____

_____

_____

_____

_____

_____

_____

_____

_____

_____

_____

21-86. Alexander Gardner. *Home of a Rebel Sharpshooter, Gettysburg.* July 1863. *(page 737)*

_____

_____

_____

_____

_____

_____

_____

_____

_____

_____

_____

Chapter Twenty-Two
Realism and Impressionism

Notes

22-1. Gustave Courbet. *Burial at Ornans.* 1849–50. *(page 739)*

22-2. Gustave Courbet. *Studio of a Painter: A Real Allegory Summarizing My Seven Years of Life as an Artist.* 1854–55. *(page 740)*

22-3. Édouard Manet. *Luncheon on the Grass (Le Déjeuner sur l'herbe)*. 1863. *(page 741)*

22-4. Édouard Manet. *The Fifer*. 1866. *(page 742)*

22-5. Claude Monet. *On the Bank of the Seine, Bennecourt*. 1868. *(page 743)*

22-6. Claude Monet. *Red Boats, Argenteuil.*
1875. *(page 743)*

_____

_____

_____

_____

_____

_____

_____

_____

_____

_____

22-7. Camille Pissarro. *The Côte des Boeufs at
l'Hermitage, near Pontoise.* 1877. *(page 743)*

_____

_____

_____

_____

_____

_____

_____

_____

_____

_____

_____

_____

_____

22-8. Auguste Renoir. *Luncheon of the Boating
Party, Bougival.* 1881. *(page 744)*

_____

_____

_____

_____

_____

_____

_____

_____

_____

_____

22-9. Édouard Manet. *A Bar at the Folies-Bergère.*
1881–82. *(page 745)*

22-10. Edgar Degas. *The Glass of Absinthe.*
1876. *(page 747)*

22-11. Edgar Degas. *Prima Ballerina.* c. 1876.
(page 746)

22-12. Edgar Degas. *The Tub.* 1886. *(page 746)*

22-13. Berthe Morisot. *The Cradle.* 1872.
(page 748)

22-14. Mary Cassatt. *The Bath.* 1891–92.
(page 748)

22-15. Claude Monet. *Water Lilies.* 1907. *(page 749)*

22-16. Ford Madox Brown. *The Last of England.* 1852–55. *(page 750)*

22-17. William Holman Hunt. *The Awakening Conscience.* 1853. *(page 750)*

22-18. Dante Gabriel Rossetti. *Beata Beatrix.*
1872. *(page 751)*

22-19. Edward Burne-Jones. *The Wheel of
Fortune.* 1877–83. *(page 751)*

BOX. Edgar Degas. *Orchestra of the Opera.*
c. 1870. *(page 753)*

22-20. James Abbott McNeill Whistler. *Arrangement in Black and Gray: The Artist's Mother.* 1871. *(page 754)*

22-21. James Abbott McNeill Whistler. *Nocturne in Black and Gold: The Falling Rocket.* c. 1874. *(page 754)*

22-22. George Inness. *The Rainbow.* c. 1878–79. *(page 755)*

22-23. Winslow Homer. *Snap the Whip.* 1872. *(page 755)*

22-24. Thomas Eakins. *William Rush Carving His Allegorical Figure of the Schuylkill River.* 1877. *(page 756)*

22-25. Henry O. Tanner. *The Banjo Lesson.* c. 1893. *(page 757)*

22-26. Auguste Rodin. *The Man with the Broken Nose.* 1864. *(page 757)*

22-27. Auguste Rodin. *The Thinker.* 1879–89. *(page 758)*

22-28. Auguste Rodin. *The Kiss.* 1886–98. *(page 758)*

22-29. Auguste Rodin. *Monument to Balzac.*
1897–98. *(page 759)*

22-30. Camille Claudel. *Ripe Age.* c. 1907.
(page 760)

22-31. Edgar Degas. *The Little Fourteen-Year-Old Dancer.* 1878–80. *(page 760)*

22-32. Henri Labrouste. Bibliothèque Ste.-Geneviève, Paris. 1843–50 *(page 761)*

22-33. Henri Labrouste. Reading Room, Bibliothèque Ste.-Geneviève *(page 762)*

22-34. Sir Joseph Paxton. The Crystal Palace, London. 1851; reerected in Sydenham 1852; destroyed 1936 *(page 762)*

22-35. John and Washington Roebling. The Brooklyn Bridge, New York. 1867–83 *(page 763)*

_____

_____

_____

_____

_____

_____

_____

_____

_____

_____

22-36. Gustave Eiffel. The Eiffel Tower, Paris. 1887–89 *(page 764)*

_____

_____

_____

_____

_____

_____

_____

_____

_____

_____

BOX. Sarah Bernhardt. *Fantastic Inkwell, Self-Portrait As a Sphinx.* After 1880. *(page 765)*

_____

_____

_____

_____

_____

_____

_____

_____

_____

_____

_____

22-37. William Morris (Morris & Co.). Green
Dining Room. 1867. *(page 766)*

22-38. James Abbott McNeill Whistler. *Harmony
in Blue and Gold: The Peacock Room.* 1876–77.
(page 767)

Chapter Twenty-Three
Post-Impressionism, Symbolism, and Art Nouveau

Notes

23-1. Paul Cézanne. *A Modern Olympia (The Pasha)*. Early 1870s. *(page 769)*

_____

_____

_____

_____

_____

_____

_____

_____

_____

_____

_____

23-2. Paul Cézanne. *Self-Portrait*. c. 1879. *(page 770)*

_____

_____

_____

_____

_____

_____

_____

_____

_____

_____

_____

23-3. Paul Cézanne. *Still Life with Apples in a Bowl.* 1879–82. *(page 771)*

23-4. Paul Cézanne. *Mont Ste.-Victoire Seen from Bibemus Quarry.* c. 1897–1900. *(page 771)*

23-5. Georges Seurat. *A Sunday Afternoon on the Island of La Grande Jatte.* 1884–86. *(page 772)*

23-6. Georges Seurat. *The Couple.* c. 1884–85. *(page 773)*

23-7. Georges Seurat. *Chahut.* 1889–90. *(page 773)*

23-8. Henri de Toulouse-Lautrec. *At the Moulin Rouge.* 1893–95. *(page 774)*

23-9. Henri de Toulouse-Lautrec. *La Goulue.*
1891. *(page 775)*

23-10. Vincent van Gogh. *The Potato Eaters.*
1885. *(page 775)*

23-11. Vincent van Gogh. *Wheat Field and
Cypress Trees.* 1889. *(page 776)*

23-12. Vincent van Gogh. *Self-Portrait.* 1889.
(page 776)

_____

_____

_____

_____

_____

_____

_____

_____

_____

_____

_____

23-13. Paul Gauguin. *The Vision after the Sermon (Jacob Wrestling with the Angel).* 1888.
(page 777)

_____

_____

_____

_____

_____

_____

_____

_____

_____

_____

_____

BOX. Odilon Redon. *Orpheus.* c. 1903-10.
(page 778)

_____

_____

_____

_____

_____

_____

_____

_____

_____

_____

23-14. Paul Gauguin. *Where Do We Come From?*
What Are We? Where Are We Going? 1897. *(page 779)*

_____

_____

_____

_____

_____

_____

_____

_____

_____

_____

23-15. Édouard Vuillard. *The Suitor.* 1893.
(page 780)

_____

_____

_____

_____

_____

_____

_____

_____

_____

_____

_____

_____

_____

23-16. Pierre-Cécile Puvis de Chavannes. *The Sacred
Grove,* c. 1883–84; *Vision of Antiquity,* c. 1888–89; and
Christian Inspiration, c. 1888–89. *(page 781)*

_____

_____

_____

_____

_____

_____

_____

_____

_____

_____

_____

23-17. Gustave Moreau. *The Apparition (Dance of Salomé).* c. 1876. *(page 782)*

_____
_____
_____
_____
_____
_____
_____
_____
_____
_____
_____

23-18. Aubrey Beardsley. *Salomé.* 1892. *(page 783)*

_____
_____
_____
_____
_____
_____
_____
_____
_____
_____
_____
_____
_____
_____

23-19. Odilon Redon. *The Eye Like a Strange Balloon Mounts Toward Infinity,* from the series *Edgar A. Poe.* 1882. *(page 783)*

_____
_____
_____
_____
_____
_____
_____
_____
_____
_____
_____

23-20. James Ensor. *Christ's Entry into Brussels in 1889.* 1888. *(page 783)*

23-21. Edvard Munch. *The Scream.* 1893. *(page 784)*

23-22. Gustav Klimt. *The Kiss.* 1907–8. *(page 785)*

23-23. Pablo Picasso. *The Old Guitarist.* 1903. *(page 785)*

23-24. Henri Rousseau. *The Dream.* 1910. *(page 786)*

23-25. Paula Modersohn-Becker. *Self-Portrait.* 1906. *(page 786)*

23-26. Aristide Maillol. *Seated Woman (La Méditerranée).* c. 1901. *(page 787)*

_____
_____
_____
_____
_____
_____
_____
_____
_____
_____
_____

23-27. Constantin Meunier. *Bust of a Puddler.* c. 1885–90. *(page 787)*

_____
_____
_____
_____
_____
_____
_____
_____
_____
_____
_____
_____
_____

23-28. Ernst Barlach. *Man Drawing a Sword.* 1911. *(page 787)*

_____
_____
_____
_____
_____
_____
_____
_____
_____
_____
_____
_____

BOX. Henri de Toulouse-Lautrec. *Le Missionnaire.*
1894. *(page 788)*

23-29. Victor Horta. Interior Stairwell of the
Tassel House, Brussels. 1892–93 *(page 790)*

23-30. Hector Guimard. Métro Station, Paris.
1900 *(page 790)*

23-31. Anton´ Gaud´. Casa Milá Apartments, Barcelona. 1905–7 *(page 791)*

23-32. Floor plan of typical floor, Casa Milá *(page 791)*

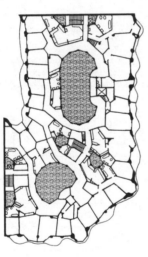

23-33. Charles Rennie Mackintosh. North facade of the Glasgow School of Art, Glasgow, Scotland. 1896–1910 *(page 791)*

23-34. Interior of the Library, Glasgow School of Art *(page 792)*

_____
_____
_____
_____
_____
_____
_____
_____
_____
_____
_____
_____

23-35. Henry van de Velde. Theater, Werkbund Exhibition, Cologne. 1914. Destroyed *(page 793)*

_____
_____
_____
_____
_____
_____
_____
_____
_____
_____
_____
_____

23-36. Plan of the Theater, Werkbund Exhibition *(page 793)*

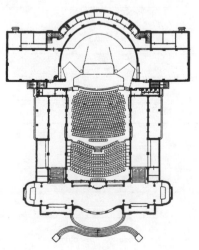

_____
_____
_____
_____
_____
_____
_____
_____
_____
_____

23-37. Henry Hobson Richardson. Marshall Field Wholesale Store, Chicago. 1885–87. Demolished 1930 *(page 793)*

BOX. Thomas Rickman and John Cragg. Interior, St. George's Church, Everton, Liverpool, England. 1812–13 *(page 795)*

23-38. Warehouses on New Quay, Liverpool. 1835–40 *(page 796)*

23-39. Louis Sullivan. Wainwright Building, St. Louis, Missouri. 1890–91. Destroyed *(page 796)*

_____
_____
_____
_____
_____
_____
_____
_____
_____
_____

23-40. Louis Sullivan. Schlesinger and Mayer Department Store, Chicago. 1899–1904 *(page 796)*

_____
_____
_____
_____
_____
_____
_____
_____
_____
_____

23-41. Detail of facade, showing window, Schlesinger and Mayer Department Store *(page 797)*

_____
_____
_____
_____
_____
_____
_____
_____
_____
_____

23-42. Jacob Riis. *Bandits' Roost.* c. 1888. *(page 797)*

23-43. Oscar Rejlander. *The Two Paths of Life.* 1857. *(page 798)*

23-44. Henry Peach Robinson. *Fading Away.* 1858. *(Page 798)*

23-45. Julia Margaret Cameron. *Ellen Terry, at the Age of Sixteen.* c. 1863. *(page 799)*

_____

_____

_____

_____

_____

_____

_____

_____

_____

_____

23-46. Peter Henry Emerson. *Haymaking in the Norfolk Broads.* c. 1890. *(page 799)*

_____

_____

_____

_____

_____

_____

_____

_____

_____

_____

_____

23-47. Gertrude Käsebier. *The Magic Crystal.* c. 1904. *(page 800)*

_____

_____

_____

_____

_____

_____

_____

_____

_____

_____

_____

23-48. Edward Steichen. *Rodin with His Sculptures "Victor Hugo" and "The Thinker."* 1902. *(page 800)*

23-49. Eadweard Muybridge. *Female Semi-Nude in Motion,* from *Human and Animal Locomotion,* vol. 2, pl. 271. 1887. *(page 801)*

23-50a and b. Étienne-Jules Marey. *Man in Black Suit with White Stripes Down Arms and Legs, Walking in Front of a Black Wall.* c. 1884. *(page 801*

Chapter Twenty-Four
Twentieth-Century Painting

Notes

24-1. Henri Matisse. *The Joy of Life.* 1905-6. *(page 803)*

_____

_____

_____

_____

_____

_____

_____

_____

_____

_____

_____

24-2. Henri Matisse. *The Red Studio.* 1911. *(page 804)*

_____

_____

_____

_____

_____

_____

_____

_____

_____

_____

_____

24-3. Georges Rouault. *Head of Christ.* 1905.
(page 805)

_____

_____

_____

_____

_____

_____

_____

_____

_____

_____

_____

24-4. Georges Rouault. *The Old King.* 1916-37.
(page 805)

_____

_____

_____

_____

_____

_____

_____

_____

_____

_____

_____

_____

_____

24-5. Ernst Ludwig Kirchner. *Self-Portrait with Model.* 1907. *(page 805)*

_____

_____

_____

_____

_____

_____

_____

_____

_____

_____

_____

24-6. Erich Heckel. *Woman Before a Mirror.* 1908. *(page 806)*

_____

_____

_____

_____

_____

_____

_____

_____

_____

_____

24-7. Emil Nolde. *The Last Supper.* 1909. *(page 806)*

_____

_____

_____

_____

_____

_____

_____

_____

_____

_____

24-8. Oskar Kokoschka. *The Bride of the Wind.* 1914. *(page 807)*

_____

_____

_____

_____

_____

_____

_____

_____

_____

_____

24-9. Vassily Kandinsky. *Sketch Ifor*
"Composition VII." 1913. *(page 808)*

_____

_____

_____

_____

_____

_____

_____

_____

_____

_____

_____

24-10. Franz Marc. *Animal Destinies.* 1913.
(page 809)

_____

_____

_____

_____

_____

_____

_____

_____

_____

_____

_____

_____

_____

24-11. Marsden Hartley. *Portrait of a German*
Officer. 1914. *(page 809)*

_____

_____

_____

_____

_____

_____

_____

_____

_____

_____

_____

_____

_____

24-12. Pablo Picasso. *Les Demoiselles d'Avignon.* 1907. *(page 810)*

24-13. Pablo Picasso. *Portrait of Ambroise Vollard.* 1910. *(page 811)*

24-14. Pablo Picasso. *Still Life with Chair Caning.* 1912. *(page 813)*

24-15. Georges Braque. *Newspaper, Bottle, Packet of Tobacco (Le Courrier).* 1914. *(page 813)*

_____

_____

_____

_____

_____

_____

_____

_____

_____

_____

24-16. Robert Delaunay. *Simultaneous Contrasts: Sun and Moon.* 1913. *(page 814)*

_____

_____

_____

_____

_____

_____

_____

_____

_____

_____

_____

24-17. Umberto Boccioni. *Dynamism of a Cyclist.* 1913. *(page 815)*

_____

_____

_____

_____

_____

_____

_____

_____

_____

_____

_____

24-18. Liubov Popova. *The Traveler.* 1915.
(page 816)

_____

_____

_____

_____

_____

_____

_____

_____

_____

_____

24-19. Kazimir Malevich. *Suprematist
Composition: White on White.* 1918. *(page 817)*

_____

_____

_____

_____

_____

_____

_____

_____

_____

_____

_____

24-20. Giorgio de Chirico. *Mystery and
Melancholy of a Street.* 1914. *(page 817)*

_____

_____

_____

_____

_____

_____

_____

_____

_____

_____

_____

BOX. Leon Bakst. *Nijinsky in L'Après-midi d'un Faune* (costume design). 1912. *(page 819)*

24-21. Marc Chagall. *I and the Village.* 1911. *(page 820)*

24-22. Marcel Duchamp. *Nude Descending a Staircase No. 2.* 1912. *(page 820)*

24-23. Marcel Duchamp. *The Bride.* 1912.
(page 821)

_____

_____

_____

_____

_____

_____

_____

_____

_____

_____

24-24. George Bellows. *Stag at Sharkey's.* 1909.
(page 821)

_____

_____

_____

_____

_____

_____

_____

_____

_____

_____

24-25. Pablo Picasso. *Three Musicians.*
Summer 1921. *(page 822)*

_____

_____

_____

_____

_____

_____

_____

_____

_____

_____

24-26. Pablo Picasso. *Mother and Child.*
1921–22. *(page 823)*

_____

_____

_____

_____

_____

_____

_____

_____

_____

_____

24-27. Pablo Picasso. *Three Dancers.* 1925.
(page 823)

_____

_____

_____

_____

_____

_____

_____

_____

_____

_____

_____

_____

_____

_____

24-28. Pablo Picasso. *Girl Before a Mirror.*
March 1932. *(page 824)*

_____

_____

_____

_____

_____

_____

_____

_____

_____

_____

_____

24-29. Pablo Picasso. *Guernica.* 1937. *(page 825)*

24-30. Henri Matisse. *Decorative Figure Against an Ornamental Background.* 1927. *(page 825)*

24-31. Ernst Ludwig Kirchner. *Winter Landscape in Moonlight.* 1919. *(page 826)*

24-32. Vassily Kandinsky. *Accented Corners, No. 247.* 1923. *(page 827)*

_____

_____

_____

_____

_____

_____

_____

_____

_____

24-33. Fernand Léger. *The City.* 1919. *(page 827)*

_____

_____

_____

_____

_____

_____

_____

_____

_____

_____

_____

24-34. Charles Demuth. *I Saw the Figure 5 in Gold.* 1928. *(page 827)*

_____

_____

_____

_____

_____

_____

_____

_____

_____

24-35. Joseph Stella. *Brooklyn Bridge.* 1917.
(page 828)

_____

_____

_____

_____

_____

_____

_____

_____

_____

24-36. Piete Mondrian. *Composition with Red, Blue, and Yellow.* 1930. *(page 829)*

_____

_____

_____

_____

_____

_____

_____

_____

_____

_____

24-37. Piet Mondrian. *Broadway Boogie Woogie.* 1942–43. *(page 830)*

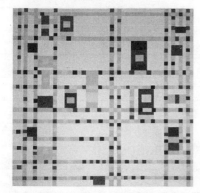

_____

_____

_____

_____

_____

_____

_____

_____

_____

24-38. Ben Nicholson. *Painted Relief.* 1939.
(page 831)

24-39. Max Ernst. *1 Copper Plate 1 Zinc Plate 1 Rubber Cloth 2 Calipers 1 Drainpipe Telescope 1 Piping Man.* 1920. *(page 831)*

24-40. Max Ernst. *La Toilette de la Mariée (The Dressing of the Bride).* 1940. *(page 832)*

24-41. Salvador Dal´. *The Persistence of Memory.* 1931. *(page 832)*

24-42. René Magritte. *Les Promenades d'Euclid.* 1955. *(page 833)*

24-43. Frida Kahlo. *Self-Portrait with Thorn Necklace.* 1940. *(page 833)*

24-44. Joan Miró. *Composition.* 1933.
(page 833)

BOX. Liubov Popova. Set design for the
Magnanimous Cuckold. 1922. *(page 835)*

24-45. Paul Klee. *Twittering Machine.* 1922.
(page 836)

24-46. Paul Klee. *Park near Lu(cerne)*. 1938.
(page 837)

_____

_____

_____

_____

_____

_____

_____

_____

_____

_____

24-47. Käthe Kollwitz. *Never Again War!* 1924.
(page 837)

_____

_____

_____

_____

_____

_____

_____

_____

_____

_____

_____

_____

24-48. George Grosz. *Germany, a Winter's Tale.*
1918. Formerly Collection Garvens, Hanover,
Germany *(page 837)*

_____

_____

_____

_____

_____

_____

_____

_____

_____

_____

_____

24-49. Max Beckmann. *The Dream.* 1921.
(page 838)

_____

_____

_____

_____

_____

_____

_____

_____

_____

24-50. Max Beckmann. *Departure.* 1932–33.
(page 839)

_____

_____

_____

_____

_____

_____

_____

_____

_____

_____

_____

24-51. Arthur G. Dove. *Foghorns.* 1929.
(page 839)

_____

_____

_____

_____

_____

_____

_____

_____

_____

_____

24-52. José Clemente Orozco. *Victims.* Detail of fresco cycle. 1936. *(page 842)*

24-53. Otto Dix. *Dr. Mayer-Hermann.* 1926. *(page 842)*

24-54. Georgia O'Keeffe. *Black Iris III.* 1926. *(page 843)*

24-55. Edward Hopper. *Early Sunday Morning.*
1930. *(page 844)*

24-56. Jacob Lawrence. *The Migration of the
Negro,* panel 3, from the series *From Every
Southern Town Migrants Left by the Hundreds to
Travel North.* 1940–41. *(page 845)*

24-57. Adolph Gottlieb. *Descent into Darkness.*
1947. *(page 845)*

24-58. Arshile Gorky. *The Liver Is the Cock's Comb.* 1944. *(page 846)*

_____

_____

_____

_____

_____

_____

_____

_____

_____

24-59. Jackson Pollock. *Autumn Rhythm: Number 30, 1950.* 1950. *(page 847)*

_____

_____

_____

_____

_____

_____

_____

_____

_____

24-60. Lee Krasner. *Celebration.* 1959–60. *(page 847)*

_____

_____

_____

_____

_____

_____

_____

_____

_____

24-61. Willem de Kooning. *Woman II.* 1952.
(page 848)

24-62. Jean Dubuffet. *Le Métafisyx,* from the
Corps de Dames series. 1950. *(page 849)*

24-63. Francis Bacon. *Head Surrounded by
Sides of Beef.* 1954. *(page 849)*

BOX. Jean Tinguely. *Hommage to New York.* 1960.
Mixed media. Self-destructing installation in the garden
of the Museum of Modern Art, New York *(page 851)*

24-64. Mark Rothko. *White and Greens in Blue.*
1957. *(page 852)*

24-65. Helen Frankenthaler. *The Bay.* 1963. *(page 852)*

24-66. Ellsworth Kelly. *Red Blue Green.* 1963.
(page 853)

24-67. Frank Stella. *Empress of India.* 1965.
(page 853)

24-68. Romare Bearden. *The Prevalence of
Ritual: Baptism.* 1964. *(page 854)*

24-69. William T. Williams. *Batman*. 1979.
(page 855)

_____
_____
_____
_____
_____
_____
_____
_____
_____
_____

24-70. Raymond Saunders. *White Flower Black Flower*. 1986. *(page 855)*

_____
_____
_____
_____
_____
_____
_____
_____
_____
_____
_____

BOX. John Cage. *Aria, Voice (any range)*.
1960. *(page 857)*

_____
_____
_____
_____
_____
_____
_____
_____
_____
_____
_____

24-71. Josef Albers. *Apparition,* from
Homageto the Square series. 1959. *(page 858)*

24-72. Richard Anuszkiewicz. *Entrance to Green.*
1970. *(page 859)*

24-73. Richard Hamilton. *Just What Is It That
Makes Today's Home So Different, So Appealing?*
1956. *(page 860)*

24-74. Jasper Johns. *Three Flags.* 1958.
(page 861)

_____

_____

_____

_____

_____

_____

_____

_____

_____

_____

_____

24-75. Roy Lichtenstein. *Drowning Girl.* 1963.
(page 861)

_____

_____

_____

_____

_____

_____

_____

_____

_____

_____

_____

_____

_____

24-76. Andy Warhol. *Gold Marilyn Monroe.*
1962. *(page 862)*

_____

_____

_____

_____

_____

_____

_____

_____

_____

_____

_____

_____

24-77. Richard Estes. *Food Shop.* 1967.
(page 863)

_____

_____

_____

_____

_____

_____

_____

_____

_____

_____

24-78. Audrey Flack. *Queen.* 1975–76.
(page 863)

_____

_____

_____

_____

_____

_____

_____

_____

_____

_____

_____

_____

24-79. Francesco Clemente. *Untitled.* 1983.
(page 864)

_____

_____

_____

_____

_____

_____

_____

_____

_____

_____

_____

24-80. Anselm Kiefer. *To the Unknown Painter.*
1983. *(page 865)*

24-81. Susan Rothenberg. *Mondrian.* 1983–84.
(page 865)

24-82. Jennifer Bartlett. *Water.* 1990. *(page 866)*

24-83. Elizabeth Murray. *More Than You Know.*
1983. *(page 867)*

_____

_____

_____

_____

_____

_____

_____

_____

_____

_____

_____

24-84. Kay WalkingStick. *On the Edge.* 1989.
(page 867)

_____

_____

_____

_____

_____

_____

_____

_____

_____

_____

_____

_____

Chapter Twenty-Five
Twentieth-Century Sculpture

Notes

25-1. Henri Matisse. *Reclining Nude I.* 1907. *(page 868)*

_____

_____

_____

_____

_____

_____

_____

_____

_____

_____

_____

25-2. Constantin Brancusi. *The Kiss.* 1909. *(page 869)*

_____

_____

_____

_____

_____

_____

_____

_____

_____

_____

_____

25-3. Constantin Brancusi. *The Newborn.* 1915.
(page 869)

_____

_____

_____

_____

_____

_____

_____

_____

_____

_____

25-4. Constantin Brancusi. *Bird in Space*
(unique cast). 1928. *(page 870)*

_____

_____

_____

_____

_____

_____

_____

_____

_____

_____

_____

25-5. Raymond Duchamp-Villon. *The Great
Horse.* 1914. *(page 870)*

_____

_____

_____

_____

_____

_____

_____

_____

_____

_____

25-6. Umberto Boccioni. *Unique Forms of Continuity in Space.* 1913. *(page 871)*

_____

_____

_____

_____

_____

_____

_____

_____

_____

_____

_____

_____

25-7. Vladimir Tatlin. *Project for Monument to the Third International.* 1919–20. *(page 872)*

_____

_____

_____

_____

_____

_____

_____

_____

_____

_____

_____

_____

_____

25-8. Naum Gabo. *Linear Construction #1* (smaller version). 1942–43. *(page 872)*

_____

_____

_____

_____

_____

_____

_____

_____

_____

_____

_____

_____

25-9. Georges Vantongerloo. *Métal: y=ax3-bx3+cx.* 1935. *(page 873)*

25-10. Jacques Lipschitz. *Figure.* 1926–30 (cast 1937). *(page 873)*

25-11. Marcel Duchamp. *In Advance of the Broken Arm.* 1945, from the original of 1915. *(page 874)*

25-12. Meret Oppenheim. *Object.* 1936.
(page 874)

_____

_____

_____

_____

_____

_____

_____

_____

_____

_____

25-13. Hans Arp. *Human Concretion.* 1935.
(page 875)

_____

_____

_____

_____

_____

_____

_____

_____

_____

_____

_____

25-14. Pablo Picasso. *Head of a Woman.* 1930-
31. *(page 875)*

_____

_____

_____

_____

_____

_____

_____

_____

_____

_____

_____

_____

25-15. Pablo Picasso. *Bull's Head.* 1943.
(page 876)

25-16. Julio González. *Head.* c. 1935. *(page 876)*

25-17. Alexander Calder. *Lobster Trap and Fish Tail.* 1939. *(page 877)*

25-18. Henry Moore. *Two Forms.* 1936.
(page 878)

_____

_____

_____

_____

_____

_____

_____

_____

_____

25-19. Henry Moore. *Recumbent Figure.* 1938.
(page 878)

_____

_____

_____

_____

_____

_____

_____

_____

_____

_____

25-20. Barbara Hepworth. *Sculpture with Color
(Deep Blue and Red).* 1940-42. *(page 879)*

_____

_____

_____

_____

_____

_____

_____

_____

_____

25-21. Mathias Goeritz. *Steel Structure.*
1952–53. *(page 879)*

25-22. Ronald Bladen. *The X* (in the Corcoran
Gallery, Washington, D.C.). 1967. *(page 880)*

25-23. David Smith. *Cubi* series (at Bolton Landing,
New York). Stainless steel. (left) *Cubi XVIII.* 1964.
(page 880)

25-24. Donald Judd. *Untitled.* 1989. *(page 881)*

_____

_____

_____

_____

_____

_____

_____

_____

_____

_____

_____

25-25. Joel Shapiro. *Untitled.* 1989-90. *(page 882)*

_____

_____

_____

_____

_____

_____

_____

_____

_____

_____

_____

25-26. Martin Puryear. *The Spell.* 1985. *(page 882)*

_____

_____

_____

_____

_____

_____

_____

_____

_____

_____

_____

25-27. Tyrone Mitchell. *Horn for Wifredo.* 1987.
(page 883)

25-28. Melvin Edwards. *To Listen.* 1990.
(page 883)

25-29. Alison Saar. *Compton Nocturne.* 1999.
(page 884)

25-30. Claes Oldenburg. *Ice Bag-Scale B.* 1970.
(page 884)

_____

_____

_____

_____

_____

_____

_____

_____

_____

_____

_____

25-31. Barnett Newman. *Broken Obelisk.* 1963–67.
(page 885)

_____

_____

_____

_____

_____

_____

_____

_____

_____

_____

_____

25-32. Isamu Noguchi. Fountain for the John
Hancock Insurance Company, New Orleans.
1961–62. *(page 886)*

_____

_____

_____

_____

_____

_____

_____

_____

_____

_____

_____

25-33. Maya Lin. *Vietnam Veterans Memorial.*
1982. *(page 886)*

25-34. Robert Smithson. *Spiral Jetty.* As built
in 1970. *(page 887)*

25-35. Christo (Christo Javacheff). *Surrounded
Islands, Project for Biscayne Bay, Greater
Miami, Florida.* 1982. *(page 888)*

25-36. Robert Rauschenberg. *Odalisk.* 1955–58.
(page 889)

_____

_____

_____

_____

_____

_____

_____

_____

_____

_____

25-37. Louise Nevelson. *Black Chord.* 1964.
(page 890)

_____

_____

_____

_____

_____

_____

_____

_____

_____

_____

_____

25-38. Barbara Chase-Riboud. *Confessions for Myself.* 1972. *(page 890)*

_____

_____

_____

_____

_____

_____

_____

_____

_____

_____

25-39. Eva Hesse. *Accession II.* 1967. *(page 891)*

25-40. George Segal. *Cinema.* 1963. *(page 891)*

25-41. Edward Kienholz. *The State Hospital.*
1966. *(page 892)*

25-42. Judy Pfaff. *Dragons.* 1965. *(page 892)*

25-43. Joseph Kosuth. *One and Three Chairs.* 1965. *(page 893)*

25-44. John Baldessari. *Art History, from Ingres and Other Parables.* 1972. *(page 894)*

25-45. Joseph Beuys. *Coyote*. Photo of performance
at Rene Block Gallery, New York, 1974 *(page 894)*

25-46. Nam June Paik. *TV Buddha*. 1974.
(page 895)

25-47. Jeff Koons. *Michael Jackson and Bubbles*.
1988. *(page 895)*

Chapter Twenty-Six
Twentieth-Century Architecture

Notes

26-1. Frank Lloyd Wright. Robie House, Chicago. 1909 *(page 897)*

_____

_____

_____

_____

_____

_____

_____

_____

_____

_____

26-2. Plan of Robie House *(page 897)*

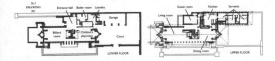

_____

_____

_____

_____

_____

_____

_____

_____

_____

_____

26-3. Frank Lloyd Wright. Installation of the living room from Francis W. Little House. The Metropolitan Museum of Art, New York *(page 897)*

26-4. Adolf Loos. Steiner House, Vienna. 1910 *(page 898)*

26-5. Peter Behrens. A.E.G. Turbine Factory, Berlin. 1909–10 *(page 898)*

26-6. Walter Gropius and Adolf Meyer. Fagus Shoe
Factory, Alfeld, Germany. 1911–14 *(page 898)*

26-7. Bruno Taut. Staircase of the "Glass House,"
Werkbund Exhibition, Cologne. 1914 *(page 899)*

26-8. Bruno Taut. The "Glass House,"
Werkbund Exhibition, Cologne. 1914 *(page 899)*

26-9. Max Berg. Interior of the Centennial Hall, Breslau, Germany. 1912–13 *(page 900)*

26-10. Antonio Sant'Elia. Central Station project for Città Nuova (after Banham). 1914 *(page 900)*

26-11. Gerrit Rietveld. Schröder House, Utrecht, Holland. 1924 *(page 901)*

26-12. Plan of the Schröder House *(page 902)*

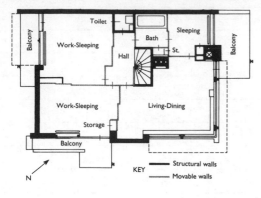

26-13. Interior, Schröder House *(page 902)*

26-14. Walter Gropius. Shop Block, the
Bauhaus, Dessau, Germany. 1925–26 *(page 903)*

26-15. Plan of the Bauhaus *(page 903)*

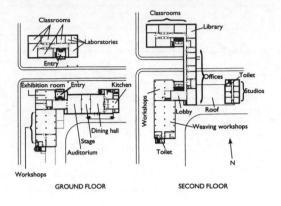

26-16. Ludwig Mies van der Rohe. German Pavilion, International Exposition, Barcelona. 1929 *(page 904)*

26-17. Ludwig Mies van der Rohe. Interior, German Pavilion *(page 904)*

26-18. Le Corbusier. Savoye House, Poissy-sur-Seine, France. 1928–29 *(page 905)*

_____

_____

_____

_____

_____

_____

_____

_____

_____

_____

26-19. Interior, Savoye House *(page 905)*

_____

_____

_____

_____

_____

_____

_____

_____

_____

_____

_____

26-20. Alvar Aalto. Villa Mairea, Noormarkku, Finland. 1937–38 *(page 906)*

_____

_____

_____

_____

_____

_____

_____

_____

_____

_____

_____

_____

26-21. Interior, Villa Mairea *(page 906)*

_____

_____

_____

_____

_____

_____

_____

_____

_____

_____

_____

26-22. Erich Mendelsohn. Einstein Tower,
Potsdam, Germany. 1921 *(page 907)*

_____

_____

_____

_____

_____

_____

_____

_____

_____

_____

_____

26-23. Auguste Perret. Notre Dame, Le Raincy,
France. 1923–24 *(page 907)*

_____

_____

_____

_____

_____

_____

_____

_____

_____

_____

_____

26-24. Marcel Breuer. The living room of Josef and Anni Albers, Masters' House, Dessau, Germany. c. 1929 *(page 907)*

26-25. Emil-Jacques Ruhlmann. Grand Salon of the Hôtel du Collectionneur at the 1925 Exposition, Paris *(page 908)*

26-26. Wirt Rowland, with Smith, Hinchman & Grylls, Associates, Inc. (Tiles designed by Thomas Dilorenzo and made by Rookwood, Cincinnati.) Main Lobby, Union Trust Company, Detroit. 1929 *(page 909)*

26-27. George Howe and William E. Lescaze.
Philadelphia Savings Fund Society Building,
Philadelphia. 1931–32 *(page 909)*

26-28. Ludwig Mies van der Rohe and Philip Johnson.
Seagram Building, New York. 1954–58 *(page 910)*

26-29. Le Corbusier. Unité d'Habitation Apartment
House, Marseilles, France. 1947–52 *(page 910)*

26-30. Le Corbusier. Isometric projection and cross section of Unité d'Habitation (after a drawing in Kenneth Frampton's *Modern Architecture*) *(page 910)*

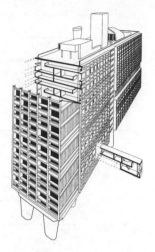

26-31. Le Corbusier. Notre-Dame-du-Haut (from the southeast), Ronchamp, France. 1950–55 *(page 911)*

26-32. Interior, Notre-Dame-du-Haut *(page 911)*

26-33. Louis Kahn. Jonas Salk Institute of Biological Studies, La Jolla, California. 1959–65 *(page 912)*

26-34. Eero Saarinen. Trans World Airlines Terminal, John F. Kennedy Airport, New York. 1956–63 *(page 912)*

26-35. Interior, Trans World Airlines Terminal, John F. Kennedy Airport *(page 912)*

26-36. Pier Luigi Nervi and Annibale Vitellozzi.
Sports Palace, Rome. 1956–57 *(page 913)*

26-37. Interior, Sports Palace, Rome *(page 913)*

26-38. Jørn Utzon with Hall, Todd, and Littlemore.
Sydney Opera House, Sydney, Australia. 1957–73
(page 914)

26-39. Frank Lloyd Wright. Solomon R. Guggenheim
Museum, New York. 1956–59 *(page 915)*

26-40. Interior of the Solomon R. Guggenheim
Museum *(page 915)*

26-41. Oscar Niemeyer. Brasilia, Brazil.
Completed 1960 *(page 916)*

26-42. Richard Meier. The Atheneum, New Harmony, Indiana. 1975–79 *(page 917)*

26-43. Gustav Peichl. Austrian Radio and Television Studio, Salzburg. 1970–72 *(page 918)*

26-44. Interior, Austrian Radio and Television Studio *(page 918)*

26-45. Richard Rogers and Renzo Piano. Centre National d'Art et Culture Georges Pompidou, Paris. 1971–77 *(page 919)*

26-46. Santiago Calatrava. TGV (Très Grande Vitesse) Super Train Station, Satolas, Lyons. 1988–94 *(page 920)*

26-47. Rem Koolhaas. Foyer of the Netherlands Dance Theater, Amsterdam. 1987. *(page 921)*

26-48. Foster Associates. Hearst Corporation,
New York. Begun 2000 *(page 921)*

_____

_____

_____

_____

_____

_____

_____

_____

_____

_____

Chapter Twenty-Seven
Twentieth-Century Photography

Notes

27-1. Louis Lumière. *Young Lady with an Umbrella.* 1906–10. *(page 922)*

27-2. Eugène Atget. *Versailles.* 1924. *(page 923)*

27-3. André Kertész. *Blind Musician.* 1921.
(page 924)

_____
_____
_____
_____
_____
_____
_____
_____
_____
_____
_____

27-4. Brassaï. *"Bijou" of Montmartre.* 1933.
(page 924)

_____
_____
_____
_____
_____
_____
_____
_____
_____
_____
_____
_____

27-5. Henri Cartier-Bresson. *Mexico, 1934.* 1934.
(page 925)

_____
_____
_____
_____
_____
_____
_____
_____
_____
_____

27-6. Alfred Stieglitz. *The Steerage.* 1907.
(page 926)

27-7. Alfred Stieglitz. *Equivalent.* 1930.
(page 927)

27-8. Edward Weston. *Pepper.* 1930. *(page 927)*

27-9. Ansel Adams. *Moonrise, Hernandez,*
New Mexico. 1941. *(page 928)*

_____

_____

_____

_____

_____

_____

_____

_____

_____

_____

27-10. Margaret Bourke-White. *Fort Peck Dam,*
Montana. 1936. *(page 929)*

_____

_____

_____

_____

_____

_____

_____

_____

_____

_____

_____

_____

27-11. Edward Steichen. *Greta Garbo.* 1928
(for *Vanity Fair* magazine). *(page 929)*

_____

_____

_____

_____

_____

_____

_____

_____

_____

_____

_____

27-12. Wayne Miller. *Childbirth.* "Family of Man" exhibition. 1955 *(page 930)*

27-13. James VanDerZee. *At Home.* 1934. *(page 930)*

27-14. Albert Renger-Patzsch. *Potter's Hands.* 1925. *(page 931)*

27-15. August Sander. *Pastry Cook, Cologne.*
1928. *(page 931)*

_____

_____

_____

_____

_____

_____

_____

_____

_____

_____

_____

27-16. Josef Sudek. *View from Studio Window in
Winter.* 1954. *(page 932)*

_____

_____

_____

_____

_____

_____

_____

_____

_____

_____

_____

27-17. Robert Capa. *Death of a Loyalist Soldier.*
September 5, 1936 *(page 932)*

_____

_____

_____

_____

_____

_____

_____

_____

_____

_____

_____

27-18. Dorothea Lange. *Migrant Mother, California.* February 1936. *(page 933)*

27-19. Herbert Bayer. *lonely metropolitan.* 1932. *(page 934)*

27-20. John Heartfield. *As in the Middle Ages, So in the Third Reich.* 1934. *(page 934)*

27-21. Man Ray. *Untitled* (Rayograph). 1928.
(page 935)

_____

_____

_____

_____

_____

_____

_____

_____

_____

_____

_____

27-22. László Moholy-Nagy. *Untitled. (page 935)*

_____

_____

_____

_____

_____

_____

_____

_____

_____

_____

_____

_____

27-23. Berenice Abbott. *Transformation of
Energy.* 1939–58 *(page 936)*

_____

_____

_____

_____

_____

_____

_____

_____

_____

_____

27-24. Aaron Siskind. *New York 2.* 1951.
(page 936)

27-25. Minor White. *Ritual Branch.* 1958.
(page 937)

27-26. W. Eugene Smith. *Tomoko in Her Bath.*
December 1971. *(page 937)*

27-27. Robert Frank. *Santa Fe, New Mexico.*
1955–56. *(page 938)*

_____

_____

_____

_____

_____

_____

_____

_____

_____

27-28. Bill Brandt. *London Child.* 1955j
(page 939)

_____

_____

_____

_____

_____

_____

_____

_____

_____

_____

_____

27-29. Jerry Uelsmann. *Untitled.* c. 1972.
(page 939)

_____

_____

_____

_____

_____

_____

_____

_____

_____

_____

_____

27-30. David Hockney. *Gregory Watching the Snow Fall, Kyoto, Feb. 21, 1983.* 1983. *(page 940)*

27-31. Joanne Leonard. *Romanticism Is Ultimately Fatal,* from *Dreams and Nightmares.* 1982. *(page 940)*

27-32. David Wojnarowicz. *Death in the Cornfield.* 1990. *(page 941)*

Chapter Twenty-Eight
Postmodernism

Notes

28-1. Michael Graves. Public Services Building, Portland, Oregon. 1980–82 *(page 945)*

_____

_____

_____

_____

_____

_____

_____

_____

_____

_____

28-2. SITE Projects, Inc., with Maple-Jones Associates. Best Stores Showroom, Houston. 1975 *(page 946)*

_____

_____

_____

_____

_____

_____

_____

_____

_____

_____

28-3. James Stirling, Michael Wilford and
Associates. Neue Staatsgalerie, Stuttgart,
Germany. Completed 1984 *(page 947)*

_____

_____

_____

_____

_____

_____

_____

_____

_____

_____

_____

28-4. Coop Himmelblau. Roof Conversion
Project, Vienna. 1983–88 *(page 948)*

_____

_____

_____

_____

_____

_____

_____

_____

_____

_____

_____

28-5. Behnisch and Partner. Hall between
Laboratory Wings, Hysolar Research Institute,
University of Stuttgart. 1987 *(page 948)*

_____

_____

_____

_____

_____

_____

_____

_____

_____

_____

_____

_____

28-6. Bernard Tschumi Architects. Folie P6,
Parc de La Villette, Paris. 1983 *(page 949)*

28-7. Frank Gehry. Guggenheim Museum,
Bilbao, Spain. 1992–97 *(page 951)*

28-8. Eric Owen Moss. A building in the complex
at Samitaur, Culver City, California. 1989–95
(page 951)

28-9. Luciano Fabro. *The Birth of Venus.* 1992.
(page 952)

28-10. Audrey Flack. *Head of Medusa.* 1990.
(page 953)

28-11. Ilya Kabakov. *The Man Who Flew into Space from His Apartment,* from "Ten Characters." 1981–88. *(page 954)*

28-12 and 28-13. Ann Hamilton. *parallel lines.* Two parts of an installation in two rooms, São Paulo Bienal, September–December 1991. *(page 955)*

28-14. Mildred Howard. *Tap: Investigation of Memory.* 1989. *(page 955)*

28-15. Pepón Osorio. *Badge of Honor.* 1995. Installation view at Ronald Feldman Fine Arts, New York, April 25–June 1, 1996, *(page 956)*

28-16. A. R. Penck. *The Demon of Curiosity.*
1982. *(page 957)*

28-17. Mark Tansey. *Derrida Queries De Man.*
1990. *(page 957)*

28-18. Barbara Kruger. *You Are a Captive
Audience.* 1983. *(page 958)*

28-19. Cindy Sherman. *Untitled Film Still #2.*
1977. *(page 959)*

_____

_____

_____

_____

_____

_____

_____

_____

_____

_____

_____

28-20. Andreas Gursky. *Paris, Montparnasse.*
1993. *(page 959)*

_____

_____

_____

_____

_____

_____

_____

_____

_____

_____

_____